Touching
Fireflies

Althea S. Palmer

ISBN 978-1-64492-071-8 (paperback)
ISBN 978-1-64492-070-1 (digital)

Christian Faith Publishing, Inc.
832 Park Avenue
Meadville, PA 16335
www.christianfaithpublishing.com

Printed in the United States of America

To my mother, Linette.

Your faith and trust in God is a testimony that when we allow God to be the master of our lives, he withholds no good thing.

"Know therefore that the Lord thy God, he is God, the faithful God, which keepeth covenant and mercy with them that love him and keep his commandments to a thousand generations" (Deuteronomy 7:9 KJV).

Contents

Immeasurable Love

Grateful

For the ripple in the shallow pond,
The morning dew that clothed the yellow daffodils,
I am grateful.
When dawn awakens
And the moon succumbs to slumber's song,
I thank you.
For the red-combed rooster's crow
That herald in each new day,
I am grateful.

I am grateful
For the blanket of snow at the feet of naked trees.
Up above the midnight sky
Bedecked with celestial diamonds,
Enamored by your sovereignty,
Gratitude abounds.

Unvarnished truth, the grandeur of your power,
Unparalleled love and mercy,
Cradled in the arms of the Almighty.
Undeserving,
Unsolicited favor.
Forever grateful.

Thy Will

When the army of doubt overwhelms me,
The arsenal of fear and anxiety cripple my thoughts.
I trust you.
Although stormy thundering clouds barricade my path,
Attacks of confusion
And the reflection of my past try to bury me,
Thy will be done in my life, Lord.

Beneath the volcanic destruction of disappointments,
Assuredly, thy will and grace prevail.
Although drowning in still deep satin dark waters,
I cling to the myriad of promises only thy will gives.

Amidst many dreams relinquished
And the aftermath of life's glacial anguish,
I remain steadfast,
Knowing victory is near
When I sit at your feet,
Waiting for your perfect will.

Who You Are

Stories of old tell of your supernatural greatness.
They call you Emmanuel,
Lord of all lords
And Prince of Peace.
Some call you Abba Father,
The Lily of the Valley,
The Bright Morning Star.
I can only tell of who you are to me.

I see the glow of your face
When the sun parades center stage.
I see your smile and beauty
In the idyllic summer panorama.
I feel the depth of your love
When I open my eyes anew each day.
I hear your voice in the wind's acoustic ballad.

You are my faithful God,
The giver of peace,
The keeper of my life,
The master of my being.
You are grace
And a wonder
Mirrored by the mystic fog
That hovers above the valleys and plains.

Messiah,
Lord,
Savior.
You are the God of old
The God of today.
To me, you are the one true God.
The God who never changes.

Extraordinary

Humble beginning,
Small island life,
Yet I still believe
My mother's faith in God
Left an indelible impression
That nothing is impossible
Because, at the opportune time,
When God steps in,
He chooses me,
Embraces me softly.
He breathes prosperity,
Then blossoms extraordinary.

Journey

Rebel heart
Raging unabated stubbornness
On the road to destruction,
And yet
You reached out and rescued me.

Unyielding heart
Shackled,
Broken,
Lost on my journey.
Still
You love me.
God loves you.

How You Love Me

You love me not because I'm perfect,
Instead
Instead you love me because of my imperfection.
You love me not because I'm worthy,
Instead
Because I seek your mercy.
You love me not because I succeed,
Instead because I fail daily.
You love me not because I am faithful,
Instead
Because I lack discipline and misconstrue the truth.
You love me not because I am strong,
Not because I am brave,
Instead
You recognize that I am weak, frail, and afraid.
You love me not because I follow your rules,
But because,
Humble on bending knees, I seek your forgiveness.
I thank you, Lord, for seeing my flaws,
Yet still
You wipe my tears.
You hold me close.
You give me peace.
You clean my slate.
No condemnation,
Instead
You love me unconditionally.

My Mother's God

In the dark, we hear you weep.
We peep through the half closed door,
See you lying on the floor,
Praying fervently,
Crying softly.

You think we are asleep.

Unaware of your distress,
Ignorant of the burden you have to bear.
Single mother,
Unemployed,
Children to feed.

Faith like Job,
Intentionally,
Consistently
Trusting God.
You are reminded,
He will never forsake you.

Consoled.

Your crying becomes
Prayer and fasting.

Praise

For all the blessings,
I lift my hands in praise.
For your unending love,
My voice echoes your praise.
My heart sings and chants your praise.
My soul testifies of your greatness.
My tears of joy,
A witness of your love for me.
Like King David, I skip, I jump,
And dance unapologetically.
For all the unseen protection,
The uncountable deliverance,
I love and adore you.
For all the wondrous things you do,
I praise you.

Somebody

I refuse to be hidden in the shadow.
I will not shudder at your piercing stare.
Ignoring all obstacles,
Armored with courage,
I exhale.
Assertively claiming
The treasures of life I truly deserve.

Poverty has no room here.
Uneducated has no victory.
Mediocrity is not an option.
Determined to finish the race I started.

I toil,
Galvanized.
Never surrender,
I claim God's destiny for me.

I am
Somebody.

Soar

Glide
High in the sky
Above the forest of clouds.
Fly beyond the heavenly bodies.
Set your goal for excellence.
Reach higher,
Surpass all expectations.

Glide,
Spread your wings wide.
Fly across the ocean,
Soar
Over the mountains,
Higher than the eagle's nest.
Waltz with success.

Sanctuary

Sometimes I lie awake in the darkness,
Quivering in tears,
Afraid about tomorrow,
Feeling weak and empty,
Then your strong voice consoles me.
You whisper in my ear.
My brokenness
Is only for a moment.
Reminds me my battles are behind me
And I already got the victory.
I fall asleep on heaven's pillow,
Safe and sheltered
In your sanctuary.

Perfect Timing

Patience fleeting,
Anxiety culminating,
Burden seeming heavy,
The journey arduous,
Time has become desperate.
Everywhere, riot of misery.
Where is hope?

Never easy waiting,
Wondering,
When is your harvest time?
Where is the bounty of your blessings?
And why is God silent?

God's timing is calculated
Not at your pace.
But his own
Sometimes he is silent as daffodils,
Yet he heard your prayer.
He is waiting for the perfect time
To open his windows
And shower you with blessings.

Redeemed

I stand in the grace of forgiveness,
As I look back in the shadow of the past.
I was chained and bound in my rebellion.
A slave on a passageway to destruction.

The promises of God must prevail.
God heard the intercessory prayers on my behalf
And broke the yoke that choked me.
He quenched my thirst
And removed the curtains of ingratitude.

Kneeling at his altar,
I submit to his call.
Rejoicing,
God has remembered even me.

Moonshine and Fireflies

Power outage,
Everywhere pitch-black.
Above
In the sky,
Smiles a full moon.
And like magic,
A spark.
Then a twinkle.
Surprise,
Fireflies.

Loving

Melody

Soft laughter,
Your charm like smooth jazz in midnight.
After dark,
When we dance,
Our bodies sway in the moonlight silhouette.

No words.
I float on the perfume of splendor of your touch.
The allure of what's to come.
You and I in musical infinity.
Intoxicated in your sweet melody.

Mystic

Footprints on wet sand,
White trails brought by the waves,
Seagulls sunbathe on isolated rocks.
From the salty water you emerge
Like the sea master of the harbor.
In that moment,
I am spellbound.

Mocha caramel, the color of your skin.
Ebony dreadlocks framed your face.
Chiseled strong cheeks,
Torso the strength of giant redwood tree.
Majestic beauty.
Again,
You look at me.
I stand in silence,
Infatuated.

Breathless

Caution halted,
Snow-clad wind swirled
Through the dense invisibility.
Piercing sapphire eyes held me captive,
Paralyzed.
No escape.
Relinquishing body and soul,
Enchanted by each touch,
Shivered by whispered kisses,
Passion intoxicated.
In a trance
Barely standing.

When You Look at Me

From my peripheral view,
I watch your stare.
Your eyes dissect me,
Do you love what you see?

Amusing,
I love how you stare,
As if I am sacred precious gemstone.
You have my permission.
Let your eyes roam and caress.

I love how you gaze at me,
Seducing
Passionately,
Like gently lover's touch.

I love how I feel
When you stare at me.

Grand Piano

Curtains up
In the spotlight.
The grand piano, a solo masterpiece.
Hidden inside it's regal frame is a network of complexity and intrigue.
Open the lid and see,
Black and white perfectly juxtaposed.
Inseparable, married for life.
From its belly bellows poetry,
Sometimes soft and mellow,
Other times whimsical and compelling.
Unspoken language, full, vibrant, and alive,
Floating on the tide of bass and treble strings.
Musically exposed
Pure heart,
Jazz, rhythm, and soul.

Hazel Eyes

Don't know what came over me.
I transformed into a pillar
When I saw those big hazel eyes.
My heart backflipped,
Then somersaulted.
Those hazel eyes struck me like a September hurricane.
Your eyes the color of lush verdant green, sunray gold,
And autumn brown enchantment.
My life took a whirlwind spin.
Nothing would ever be the same again.
I was swept away
Instantly.

Next Time

I'm going to love again,
Although enthusiasm wanes.
I will cling to the wings of optimism
And console my heart
That love will return again
Like cherry blossom in spring.

I will forget the sting of lost love
And invite pineapple nectar, ginger, and cinnamon kisses.
I wait patiently to bathe in the fortune of love,
Knowing one day
Love will venture my way.
Then I will love again.
This time, with no boundaries
But love fiercely.

Abyss

I'm drowning.
My life is disappearing.
Crippled by heartache
Haunting my nights,
Terrorizing my days.

I'm falling deeper,
Plunging further in this nightmare.
My existence, a mirage,
Isolated,
Desperately lonely.

Crippled by the hurt and pain.
I'm suffocating.
Dread overshadows,
Lingering,
The abyss prevails.

Melancholy Song

She hears her soul mourns,
Terrified of the thought of being alone.
No longer ignoring the inevitable,
Acknowledging love standing still at a roadblock.
The constant uncertainty,
The terrifying thoughts of never seeing his face every day.
No more love song.
No more long summer walks on the boardwalk.
No more admiring foliage in the fall.
She wipes away tears,
Clinging steadfast to courage,
Recognizing it is wise to walk away.

Closed Doors

Night falls
Unannounced.
Death removes its shadowy camouflage,
Floating on the grim of silence.
Surrounded by the fangs of helplessness,
A deal nonnegotiable.
The escape route impassable,
Death venomously robs and steals
The cords of one's life.
The door slammed closed.
What remains:
Haunting regrets of time not spent.

Unparallel

This is not farewell.
I can never say goodbye.
Your laughter lingers
When I close my eyes.
Still see your wide grin
And your mischievous chuckle,
You will remain my first true love.

Although the road map of life has redirected our path,
The music stopped.
Our waltz complete,
Still no goodbyes here.
I will cherish the memories of what it means to be truly loved.
This is not farewell.
Sleep, Daddy, till next we meet.

Leopard Heels

Black leather sequined jacket,
Unbuttoned.
Snow white T-shirt
Peeped through.
My breast heaved with every breath.
My hips hugged
In a high waist Aegean blue denim jeans.

I walk slowly,
Silhouetted against the dimly lit chandelier.
I caught his eyes,
Annoyingly persistently,
Undressing me
When I enter the room
In my six-inch leopard heels.

No nylon stocking,
No gold, diamonds, or pearls,
Only fresh freckled face.
Scent of rosewater perfume
And cranberry ruby red lips.
He watched me
As I strut across the floor
In my six-inch leopard heels.

Gasping with apprehension,
He walked over to me.
Greeted by his wide handsome grin,
He said hello.
His warm breath kisses my cheek
When he whispers in my ear,
"You cast a spell on me in those six-inch leopard heels."

Vulnerable

In your eyes, I look fearless,
Always seem in total control.
You see courage,
The unconquerable giant,
The coveted summit,
Unreachable.
The red-breasted swallow that glides high above the mountains
And to the clouds.

In your eyes, you see confidence.
The engine that keeps running,
Unstoppable me.
No insecurity.
I am the river pebble.
I skip and dance on the surface of the green-blue roaring river.
Never sinks.
I am the feather that floats on the voices of the wind.
I never touch the ground.

Oh so wrong.
I, too, taste the bitterness of disappointment.
I listen to sad songs and jazz.
At nightfall,
Blinds closed,
In the dark, I cry.
Sometimes I feel invisible,
Trekking on a road less traveled.
I am the book with torn covers,
Crumpled and missing pages.
You see perfection,

Secrets unfold,
Peel away the image you have of me.
Look closely
And see me.

Love of Country

I See Jamaica

My ears popped as the altitude dropped.
I opened my eyes.
Down below, the deep blue sea,
From my breath-misted window pane,
I see Jamaica.

Clothed in luscious green mountains that caress the sky,
With mystic valleys that hide the secrets of Jamaica's rich history,
I long to feel the seductive Caribbean breeze pinch my cheeks.
Unexplainable, the sensation that surges through my veins
When I see Jamaican land.
The place I truly belong.

I reminisce on the aroma of ripe fruits in the summer,
Sitting on the verandah, watching the flight of the hummingbird.
While in the distance, little boys frolicked in the river.
Their mothers sing folk song
With hands akimbo.

It will not be long.
Down below,
Jamaica awaits me.

Waterloo

Still dawn,
The moon enveloped in dark clouds,
Dogs roam the alleys like disorganized militia.
Music stopped,
The dance locked down,
Revelers stomping the city streets.
Loosely clad ladies
With their effervescent-colored costumes,
Sweat sparkles on their skin.
Men cursing and laughing,
Their faces lost in thick ganja smoke.
In the rubble on the sidewalk,
Homeless men sleeping covered
Under sheets of cardboards.
At the intersection of Old Hope Road and Waterloo,
The traffic light changed to red.
The warm crisp breeze hums melodiously
At the corner.
The rastaman shouts,
"Gleaner! Gleaner!"
Green light,
Time to go.

Mango Walk

Summertime,
No raincloud in sight.
Only the bold raging sun
Unleashing its wrath.

Soaked in sweat,
Catch shade under the lignum vitae tree,
Getting ready for mango picking

Crocus bag in hand,
Cross the riverbank,
Bending and crawling on the narrow trail.

Machete chopping the overgrown shrubs and bushes,
Crawling under the barbed wire fence,
Careful not to get caught
Ahead,
Welcomed by sweet mango scent.

Hundreds and hundreds of heavy-laden mango trees,
Unsure where to start.
Mango green,
Mango yellow,
Red mango,
Sweet mango.

Face stained with mango nectar,
Belly full,
Feeling content.
Time to cross the riverbank again.

October Flood

Hurricane season again.
The trees sway and bend,
Hammered from the storm's wind.
Rain like bullet pellets,
Hitting the roof like bullets ricocheting from a gang fight.
Leaves and debris scattered about.
No school.
No work.
Everything locked down.

Excitement surge.
Waves of chocolate brown water
Overflow the gully's banks.
The street under sieged,
Leaving families hostage.
Furniture high in the ceiling placed on concrete blocks,
Sandbags barricade doors.
Everyone prepared,
Frustrated and afraid,
Remembering the flood's destruction from last year.

October rain brings
October flood.

Pepper Pot Soup

I am pepper pot soup.
A little bit of this,
A little bit of that.
My father's eyes,
My nanna's nose,
My burnt amber shade hair,
Mirrors that of my great-grandmother,
My great-grandfather's smile,
And my mother's steady long stride.

I am pepper pot soup.
A combination of food
In a one-pot meal.
A cup of Ivory Coast,
Togo and Cameroon,
Half a cup of Senegal and Congo,
And a teaspoon of Italy, Greece, and Finland,
And a pinch of Middle East.
My identity.

I am pepper pot.
I am African.
I am Jamaican.

Pick di Road

Raindrops beat like bass drums on zinc roof.
Coconut trees dance and prance effortlessly in the strong wind.
Towering banana trees topple like giants to the ground.
Ripe plums and breadfruit burst and scattered all about.
What was once a dusty unpaved road,
Now hidden under streams of muddy water.

Mummy seh unu pick di road dis mawning
Unu tek out di raincoat dem
Nuh step inna di dutty wata
Look out fi di pot ole dem
An mek sure unu walk pon di bankin
Watch out fi di mad driva dem
Nuh mek dem splash di wata pon yu tunic
Shi tell mi brother roll up you khaki pant till when you reach a school.

The gate close behind us.
Through the aluminum window,
Mommy shouts for the last time,
"Memba fi pic di road."

Half Way Tree and Town

Half Way Tree,
Cross Roads, and Town.
Cum, brown man.
Cum, nice lady.
A Thursday
Ben Johnson day
Unu nah go a town.

The conductor clings to di open window
Standing on the bus step
Im body hanging out di bus
Look lik him nuh know danger
Unu come nuh
A town wi a go
School pickney hurry up
Cum granny
Nuff seat inna di bus
Half Way Tree,
Cross Roads, and Town.
Unu step up inna di bus.

Half Way Tree,
Cross Roads, and Town.
Pretty lady, yu nah cum.
Di lady shake ar ead and wipe di sweat off ar forehead.
Di sun tan up inna massa Gad clear blue sky,
Like a a soldja pon duty uppa Up-park camp.
Cum pretty lady, cum outta di sun.
Yuh nah go town.
Di lady shake ar ead an retreat ina di shade.

Yuh gwaan, a yuh man yuh a wait pon
Shatta driva
Shi nah go nuh whey.

Half Way Tree,
Cross Roads, and Town.
Cum, baby madddda.
A Busta Aspital yuh a go
Mek mi elp yuh.
A nuff seat inna di bus.
Come, baby madda.
Nuh mek yuh pretty baby bun up inna di sun
Unu small up unu self an gi di baby madda a seat
Ey big bredren inna di red shirt
Nuh badda block di way
Yu a tek up too much space.

Half Way Tree,
Cross roads, and Town.
Cum, brown man.
Cum, nice lady.
A Thursday
Ben Johnson day
Unu nah go a town.

Croco Lizard

Every night, the croco lizard crawls out from his hiding place.
Under the zinc roof,
Behind the wardrobe, his favorite spots.
Tonight, he is crawling
From behind the picture frame on the wall.
His gray-ash brown face peeped out.
His beady black eyes stick to the side of his face
Like pimento seed.
He has escaped death numerous times,
So with caution,
He slowly ventures out.

The croco lizard never comes out during the day.
When night falls,
He mysteriously appears.
He camouflages himself with the concrete slab ceiling,
Foraging for light bugs, flies, mosquitoes.
He never appears afraid.
He is always alone.
He comes and goes as he likes.
He is never in a rush.

Country Girl

Little country girl,
You run barefoot all day long
Into the belly of the parched dry riverbed,
Into the shadow of the ramshackle bridge.
Your heavy breathing escapes your lungs,
Chiming as you carry along.
No time to rest.
You gallop down the valley of tall elephant grass
Beneath the midsummer eventide.

Little barefoot country girl,
You trek relentlessly
On the trail ahead,
With gravel under your toes.
Feet stained, baked red-brown
By the winding dirt road.
No time to rest.
You keep trudging forward,
With the hurling wind behind your shoulders.

Little country girl,
Aren't you tired yet?
You have no harness or limits.
You run swiftly with wings of the hummingbird,
Soaring effortlessly with the sparrows.
Unashamedly, fearlessly,

You summit the rocky hill like a mountain goat.
What are you searching for
When you run barefoot all day long?

8115 Vilakazi Street, Orlando West, Soweto

Late September,
Pleasantly crispy clear morning breeze.
Tiptoe across my cheeks,
I step out of the car.
Inhale deeply.
Savor the sweet aroma of the warm Dombolo,
Spicy Chakalaka, Kota, and Mogudu,
Knowing this day
Will forever be engraved in my memory
As I walk slowly up
The slight slope toward
8115 Vilakazi Street.

Pulling long braids from my face,
Ahead,
My destination.
The place Nelson Mandela
Once called home.
Excitement surge through my veins,
My heart throbs,
The beat of Djembe drum,
I dance
To the symphony of the African sun,
Becoming a pronking springbok,
Enjoying the merriment
Of the pantsula dancers,
Hoping to blend in
As a local of Soweto.

Overwhelmed by emotions,
Guffaw, laughter
Erupt into flowing tears.
My heart swells with joy.
Today is victory
Because I stand on the grounds
Where the bravest
And the strongest man lived.
I enter the small humble house.
Run my fingers across maroon brick wall.
I find myself wondering
When Mandela sat under this tree
In his front garden.
Did he see freedom?

I bent down in the yard,
Listening to the chants
Of colorful Soweto.
My eyes shut.
I envision the good days
When Nelson Mandela's children played
Under the watchful eyes of young Winnie Mandela
Before the darkness
Of apartheid's segregation.

Today is victory
Because I walk on the grounds
Where the bravest
And the strongest man lived.
Here on continent Africa,
Land of my ancestors,
I smile,
Knowing I will never forget.

Today is victory,
As I walk slowly
Down Vilakazi Street, Orlando West,
Soweto.

Salt River, Tuesday Evening

The sun retires behind the hills
To take an afternoon nap.
The tiny yellow-faced grassquit sings sweetly,
Perched on a limb of the lignum vitae's
Hiding shade.
A shelter from the scorching hot July day.

The mangrove forest stood like brave soldiers,
Roots dense and tangled in a maze.
The clear water
Gushes from the stone wall
Into a pool of inviting, glistening saltwater.

Submerged head deep
After a whooping plunge
Into the natural mineral spring,
Eyes sting and burn.
Tinged red by the coastal saline,
Lick salty lips.
Skin smears with deposits of silt
Resembles body painting.
Early morning at J'Ouvert.

Beneath the slow moving water,
Toes sink in a spongy mud bed.
Curious fishes nibble at your heels.
Conical reddish-brown berries
Fall from the mangrove trees.
Floating about with shrubs,

Fine bamboo.
Brown, green, and yellow leaves.

Every Tuesday evening
When the day gets maddening hot,
Sweat rolling down your back
Like Dunn's river falls.
Escape the blistering heat
With a refreshing dip
In the cool colors of
Clarendon's salt river.

Island Life

I feel so at home
When I walk along the shoreline.
Free from urban chaos,
A welcome escape from the intensity of technological invasion,
Emerged into the paradise of rustic island life,
Lignum vitae blooms.
Nightingale hums and buzzes,
Sucking on the sweet pomegranate and mango.

I feel at home.
Cold beer in hand.
Sugar-white powdered sand tickle my toes,
Sun-kissed skin sparkle and tingle,
Basking into luminous calm,
Watching the soft white frills of the waves
Caress the gray-black rocks,
Listening to the tides,
And the breeze in symphony.

I feel at home
Greeted by the smiles from a perfect stranger,
Surrounded by the kaleidoscope of turquoise blue,
And emerald green of the Caribbean Sea.
As I quench my thirst with coconut jelly,
Lost in the all too familiar scene of people
Who look and speak like me.
Men laughing under almond tree,
Slamming dominos,

Drinking white rum,
I lower my anchor
And sink deeply into paradise.

Home again
At last.

"The Lord hath appeared of old unto me saying, 'Yea, I have loved thee with an everlasting love, therefore with loving kindness have I drawn thee'" (Jeremiah 31:3, KJV).

About the Author

Althea S. Palmer is a nurse practitioner and adjunct nursing professor. She was born in St. Andrew, Jamaica, and considered herself *a forever small island girl.* She lives in Long Island, New York.

Driven by wanderlust, she is a globe-trekker, seeking the next adventure, including connecting with people, places, and cultures.

Althea's love for writing began in her childhood when she spent many summer days writing poetry, story-telling, and reading. Her poetry has been published in the *The Gleaner Jamaica*, West Indies, Fairleigh Dickinson University Literary Magazine, *Knightscapes*, and *Twilight Musing*, a compilation of poetry by The International Library of Poetry.

This is Althea's first book of poetry.

CPSIA information can be obtained
at www.ICGtesting.com
Printed in the USA
FSHW010621140320